EZRA, NEHEMIAH, ESTHER

ingdom) 931 *(See pages 14–16)*

• Israel falls to Assyria 722

• Gedaliah, governor of Judah 586

• Judah falls to Babylon; temple destroyed; people exiled 586

Habakkuk c. 609–598

Malachi c. 400s

Daniel c. 605–535

Joel (dates unknown)

Ezekiel c. 593–571

753

Obadiah c. 586

• Cyrus allows Jews to return from exile 538

c. 760–753

1 and 2 Kings written c. 561–539

• Rebuilding of the temple begins 536

a c. 752–722

Haggai c. 520

Zechariah c. 520–518

Micah c. 738–698

• Zerubbabel and Joshua the high priest; temple completed 516

Isaiah c. 735–681

Nahum c. 663–612

Queen Esther c. 478

Ezra goes to Judah 457 •

Zephaniah c. 641–628

1 and 2 Chronicles written c. 450–400

Jeremiah c. 626–582

Nehemiah governs Judah 444–432

Nehemiah returns to Babylon c. 432–430

Lamentations written c. 586

Ezra and Nehemiah written c. 400s

prophesied.

700 BC | 600 BC | 500 BC | 400 BC

ab c. 850

The Cyrus Cylinder tells of King Cyrus's decree allowing captives to return to their homelands and restore their temples.

Gautama Buddha of India c. 563–483

• Aesop's Fables c. 560

701

Cyrus the Great, King of Persia 559–530

mpic games

Philosopher Confucius of China 551–479

of Rome 753

• Babylon falls to Persia 539

• Darius the Mede rules Babylon 539

Assyria rules Egypt 671–652

• Roman Republic established 509

• Nineveh, capital of Assyria, falls to Babylonians and Medes 612

Athenian leader Pericles of Greece c. 500–429

King Nebuchadnezzar II of the Neo-Babylonian Empire 604–562

King Xerxes I (Ahasuerus) of Persia 485–465

King Sargon II of Assyria

King Artaxerxes of Persia 464–424

Peloponnesian War between Athens and Sparta begins 431 •

The Days of Creation

DAY 1: Light

DAY 2: Sky

DAY 3: Seas, dry land, plants

DAY 4: Sun, moon, stars

DAY 5: Fish, birds

DAY 6: Animals, humans

DAY 7: God rests

God creates the world and everything in it. Gen. 1:1–2:25

- Adam and Eve eat the forbidden fruit, sin the world, and they are banished from t Garden of Eden. *Gen. 3:1–24*
- Cain murders Abel. *Gen. 4:1–16*
- The human race multiplies and sinfulne increases. *Gen. 6:1–7*
- God instructs Noah to build an ark. *Gen*
- God sends a flood which destroys eve except Noah, his family, and the ani ark. *Gen. 7:6–8:19*
- God sends a rainbow as a sign of his with Noah. *Gen. 8:20–9:17*
- God confuses the peoples' languag tower of Babel. *Gen. 11:1–9*

JOSEPH

- Joseph's jealous brothers sell him into slavery. *Gen. 37:1–35*
- In Egypt, Joseph becomes a slave of Potiphar, a captain of Pharaoh's guard. *Gen. 37:36*
- Potiphar's wife falsely accuses Joseph and he is thrown into prison. *Gen. 39:1–20*
- Joseph interprets dreams in prison and then Pharaoh's dream. *Gen. 40:1–41:40*
- Joseph is made an official in Egypt. *Gen. 41:41–43*
- Joseph's brothers travel from Canaan to Egypt to buy food during a famine. *Gen. 42:1–3*
- Joseph tests his brothers, reveals his identity, and forgives them. *Gen. 44:1–45:14*
- Jacob's family settles in Egypt. *Gen. 46:1–7*
- Jacob blesses his sons before his death. *Gen. 49:1–28*
- Joseph dies in Egypt at 110 years old. *Gen. 50:22–26*

1800 BC **1700**

OLD TESTAMENT

Law

Genesis through Deuteronomy – 5 books

These books contain stories from the creation of the world to the time just before the Israelites entered the Promised Land. They also record God's law for the Israelites concerning sacrifice, worship, and daily living. Also called the Pentateuch (Greek, *penta*, meaning "five") and the Torah (Hebrew, meaning "instruction").

History

Joshua through Esther – 12 books

These books narrate God's activity in the lives of his people from the time they entered the Promised Land through the eras of judges, kings, exile from the land, and the return to the land.

Poetry & Wisdom

Job through Song of Songs – 5 books

These books include songs, proverbs, poems, and dramas. They illustrate the creative ways the people of Israel expressed themselves to God and to each other.

Major Prophets

Isaiah through Daniel – 5 books

These books are called *major* because of their long length. These prophets brought God's message of warning of judgment, hope for the future, and the promise of the coming Messiah.

Minor Prophets

Hosea through Malachi – 12 books

These books are called *minor* because of their short length. Like the major prophets, these twelve prophets brought God's word to the people about judgment and hope.

GENESIS

The beginnings of creation, the nations, and the Israelites

Written: c. 1446–1406 BC by Moses

Purpose: To show that God is sovereign and loves his creation.

Summary: The book of Genesis (meaning "to be born") is a book of origins: the good creation of the world, the start of human problems, and the beginning of God's solution to those problems. The stories in Genesis reveal deeply broken relationships: separation between God and his creation; rivalries among family members; and violence between people groups. Yet we also see God beginning to restore the brokenness by choosing a family—Abraham's family—and guiding and rescuing them along the way.

Outline:

The beginning of the world (1–2)

- Days of creation (1)
- First man and woman (2)

The beginning of nations (3–10)

- Adam and Eve, and the fall (3)
- Cain and Abel and their descendants (4)
- Noah and the great flood (5–9)
- The tower of Babel (10)

The beginning of the Israelites (11–50)

- Abraham, Sarah, Hagar, Isaac, Ishmael (11–24)
- Isaac, Jacob (Israel), Esau (25–36)
- Joseph (37–50)

Ur, Abraham's hometown (Genesis 11), was a powerful cultural center in the time of Abraham. The Royal Standard of Ur (shown here) was discovered in an ancient cemetery in modern Iraq, south of Baghdad.

Key Verse: *The Lord said to Abraham: "I will establish my covenant as an everlasting covenant between me and you and your descendants."* —Genesis 17:7

EXODUS

God's deliverance of the Israelites from slavery in Egypt

Written: c. 1446–1406 BC by Moses

Purpose: To show God's faithfulness to the covenant and provide Israel with guidelines for holy living.

Summary: The book of Exodus (meaning "going out") tells the story of God's people moving from bondage to freedom. God chooses a man named Moses to lead the Israelites (Hebrews) out of slavery in Egypt and into the wilderness where they can worship God. The God of Israel proves himself to be the only true God, defeating the false gods of Egypt. At Mt. Sinai, God gives his people instructions on how to live as a community of holy people.

Outline:

Israel in Egypt (1–15)

- Israelites enslaved in Egypt (1–2)
- Moses and the burning bush (3–6)
- Ten plagues and first Passover (7–12)
- The exodus and the parting of the Red Sea (13–14)

Israel on the way toward Sinai (15–18)

- Manna and quail (15–16)
- Water from a rock (17–18)

Israel at Sinai (19–40)

- The Ten Commandments; and the law (19–31)
- The golden calf (32)
- The tabernacle (33–40)

St. Catherine's Monastery (shown here) lies at the base of Mount Moses, the traditional site of Mount Sinai (Exodus 19).

Key Verse: *"God said to Moses, 'I AM WHO I AM.' This is what you are to say to the Israelites: 'I AM has sent me to you.'"* —Exodus 3:14

 LEVITICUS

Law and sacrifice

Written: c. 1446–1406 BC by Moses

Purpose: To instruct Israel on how to be holy and be a blessing to others.

Summary: The book of Leviticus (named after the tribe of Levi) teaches the Israelites how to live in the presences of a holy God. It is a detailed list of instructions for priests, purity rituals, and how to make atonement for the people's sins. The atonement made through sacrifices in Leviticus foreshadows Jesus' own sacrifice of himself on the cross that makes atonement for our sins today.

Outline:

- Sacrifice (1–7)
- Priesthood (8–10)
- Clean and unclean (11–15)
- Day of Atonement (16)
- Laws for daily life (17–27)

Key Verse:

"Consecrate yourselves and be holy, because I am the LORD your God."
—Leviticus 2:7

 NUMBERS

Census and history of the Israelites in the wilderness

Written: c. 1446–1406 BC by Moses

Purpose: To remind the people about the consequences of rebelling against God.

Summary: The book of Numbers (named after the two censuses in the book) is a story of rebellion and disobedience coupled with God's grace and mercy. The book narrates the forty years the Israelites spent in the wilderness. God punishes his people when they rebel, but he does not destroy them. He preserves them and extends grace to the next generation who would enter the land he had promised to them.

Outline:

- First census and laws (1–9)
- Travels from Sinai to Canaan (10–12)
- The spies and the rebellion (13–25)
- Second census (26)
- Israelites in Moab (27–36)

Key Verse:

The LORD bless you and keep you; the LORD make his face shine on you and be gracious to you."
—Numbers 6:24–25

DEUTERONOMY

Moses' final sermons

Written: c. 1446–1406 BC by Moses

Purpose: To remind those who would enter the Promised Land what God expects from them.

Summary: After forty years in the wilderness, the people arrive in Moab at the border of the Promised Land. The book of Deuteronomy (meaning "second law") is a series of speeches Moses gave on the plains of Moab to challenge the younger generation to find their identity and purpose in their covenant with God.

Outline:

- Sermon 1: Journey Review (1–4)
- Sermon 2: Laws (5–28)
- Sermon 3: Covenant (29–30)
- Farewells and Moses' death (31–34)

Key Verse:

"Hear, O Israel: The LORD our God, the LORD is one. Love the LORD your God with all your heart and with all your soul and with all your strength."
—Deuteronomy 6:4–5

JOSHUA

History of the conquest of the Promised Land

Written: c. 1300s BC by an unknown author (possibly Joshua or Samuel)

Purpose: To assure the people that obedience to God is rewarded.

Summary: The book of Joshua (named after the man who succeeded Moses) is the story of how God brought his people into the land he had promised to them and gave them rest.

Outline:

- Conquest of the land (1–12)
- Dividing the land among the Israelite tribes (13–22)
- Joshua's farewell address (23–24)

Key Verse: *"Be strong and very courageous. Be careful to obey all the law my servant Moses gave you; do not turn from it to the right or to the left, that you may be successful wherever you go."*
—Joshua 1:7

JUDGES

Cycles of sin and deliverance in the Promised Land

Written: c. 1350–1000 BC by an unknown author (possibly Samuel)

Purpose: To stress the importance of remaining loyal to God.

Summary: After the tribes of Israel settled in the Promised Land, they began a rapid moral and spiritual decline. But even in times when they turn their back to God and suffer the consequences, he is filled with compassion and mercy. When the people cry out to God, he raises up leaders (called judges) to deliver his people from oppression and usher in a period of peace. Yet after a while, the people would begin to do evil again, and the cycle would begin anew.

Outline:

Reasons for failure (1–2)

The Judges (3–16)

- Othniel, Ehud, Shamgar (3)
- Deborah (4–5)
- Gideon (6–9)
- Tola, Jair, Jephthah, Ibzan, Elon, Abdon (10–12)
- Samson (13–16)
- Days of lawlessness (17–21)

Key Verse: *"In those days Israel had no king; everyone did as they saw fit."* —Judges 21:25

Widespread idol worship among the Canaanites who lived in the Promised Land made it challenging for the God's people to remain faithful to worshiping only the one true God. Plaques of the Canaanite goddesses Asherah and Astarte (c. 13th–10th century BC) are shown here.

RUTH

A story of a faithful foreigner

Written: c. 1350–1000 BC by an unknown author (possibly Samuel)

Purpose: To demonstrate the faithfulness and kindness that God desires for us.

Summary: Ruth's story is set during the era of judges, a time of moral and spiritual decay. Both Naomi (an Israelite) and her daughter-in-law Ruth (a Moabitess) become widowed and fall into poverty. Naomi returns from Moab to Bethlehem, and Ruth, in faithfulness to Naomi, insists that she go with Naomi to live with the Israelites and make their God her God. In Bethlehem, Ruth, "a woman of noble character" (3:11), meets Boaz, a man of kindness. Boaz, who is a relative of Naomi, accepts the role of guardian-redeemer, and marries Ruth and buys back Naomi's land.

The book ends by informing readers that Boaz and Ruth are ancestors of King David (4:17–22). But this story is actually part of a much larger story: they are also ancestors of Jesus our Savior—the ultimate guardian-redeemer (Matthew 1:5).

When an Israelite experienced hard times, his nearest relative was required to be a guardian-redeemer, buying the land of the needy relative to prevent it from becoming the possession of someone outside the clan (Leviticus 25:25).

Outline:

- Naomi returns to Bethlehem with Ruth. (1)
- Ruth meets Boaz. (2)
- Ruth seeks out Boaz to be the guardian-redeemer. (3)
- Boaz marries Ruth. (4)

Key Verse: *Ruth replied to Naomi, "Your people will be my people and your God my God."* —Ruth 1:16

In Bible times, Bethlehem, which means "house of bread," was a small village known for its wheat and barley fields. It is the setting for the story of Ruth, the hometown of David, and the birthplace of Jesus.

1 SAMUEL

Events from the end of the judges through Israel's first king

Written: c. 1100–931 BC by an unknown author

Purpose: To record how Israel got a king.

Summary: Named after Samuel—a prophet and Israel's last judge—the book of 1 Samuel shows God's hand in history during the transition from the era of the judges through the reign of Israel's first king. When the Israelites enter the Promised Land, they are a loose collection of tribes with God as their King, but they are not satisfied. They want a king like the other nations. God grants their request in King Saul, but God eventually rejects Saul because Saul does not heed God's instructions. God then chooses a young shepherd named David to lead his people.

Outline:

Samuel (1–7)

- Hannah and her son Samuel (1–3)
- Samuel confronts the Philistines (4–7)

Saul (8–15)

- Saul becomes king (8–12)
- Saul's reign as king (13–14)
- God rejects Saul (15)

David (16–31)

- Samuel anoints David as king (16)
- David kills Goliath the Philistine (17)
- David and Saul (18–30)
- Saul dies in battle with the Philistines (31)

The Philistines lived in the southern costal region of Canaan and often fought against their Israelite neighbors and other nations. A relief (shown here) at the temple of Ramses III in Egypt depicts the Philistines as one of the "Sea Peoples" who battled the Egyptians in the 11th century BC.

Key Verse: *Samuel replied to Saul: "Does the LORD delight in burnt offerings and sacrifices as much as in obeying the LORD? To obey is better than sacrifice."* —1 Samuel 15:22

2 SAMUEL

Events during the reign of King David

Written: c. 1100–931 BC by an unknown author

Purpose: To record King David's victories and also his failures.

Summary: Like I Samuel, this second book illustrates both God's blessing upon the faithful and the disastrous consequences of sin. Though chosen and blessed by God, King David forgets that God is the ultimate King. After David commits adultery with Bathsheba and murders her husband Uriah, family violence and national rebellion soon follow. Yet we also see God's mercy, as God forgives David when he repents, preserves his kingdom in the end, and chooses to use David's royal lineage to one day bring about the Messiah, Jesus our Savior.

Outline:

David's reign in Judah (1–4)

David's reign over Israel (5–10)

- David is made king of Israel (5–6)
- God's covenant with David (7)
- David's victories (8–10)

David's sin and family strife (11–24)

- David commits adultery and murder (11)
- David repents (12)
- David's son Absalom leads a rebellion (13–18)
- David's final battles (19–24)

Originally, 1 and 2 Samuel were one book, but Greek translators in the 3rd century BC could not fit the long book onto one scroll, so they separated it into two parts. The books of Kings and Chronicles were also divided for the same reason.

Key Verse: *God's promise to David: "I have been with you wherever you have gone. . . . Now I will make your name great, like the names of the greatest men on earth."*
—2 Samuel 7:9

1 KINGS

King Solomon's reign and the division of the kingdom

Written: c. 561–539 BC by an unknown author

Purpose: To demonstrate the value of obeying God and the danger of disobeying.

Summary: Originally one book with 2 Kings, this first book covers King Solomon's impressive achievements: wise governing, completion of the temple in Jerusalem, and expansion of the kingdom. The book also explains his eventual downfall: marrying many foreign wives and worshiping their gods. After Solomon's death, civil war tears the kingdom apart.

Outline:

- King Solomon's reign (1–10)
- The kingdom splits (11–16)
- Elijah's ministry (17–22)

Key Verse: *Solomon asks God: "Give your servant a discerning heart to govern your people and to distinguish between right and wrong."* —1 Kings 3:9

2 KINGS

The slow collapse of the kingdoms of Israel and Judah

Written: c. 561–539 BC by an unknown author

Purpose: To demonstrate the value of obeying God and the danger of disobeying.

Summary: The book of 2 Kings records the history of the kings of the northern kingdom (Israel) and the southern kingdom (Judah). Despite occasional spiritual reforms—such as King Hezekiah's and King Josiah's reforms—the sins of Israel and Judah eventually result in their kingdoms being conquered and their people exiled by the Assyrian and Babylonian Empires.

Outline:

- Elisha's ministry (1–8)
- Kings of Israel and Judah (9–16)
- Fall of Israel (17)
- Hezekiah, Josiah; fall of Judah (18–25)

Key Verse: *King Hezekiah's prayer: "LORD, the God of Israel . . . you alone are God over all the kingdoms of the earth."* —2 Kings 19:15

1 CHRONICLES

The reign of King David

Written: c. 450–400 BC by an unknown author (possibly Ezra)

Purpose: To encourage the exiles who returned to Judah.

Summary: Originally one book with 2 Chronicles, this first book is a history (or chronicle) of King David's reign. Both 1 and 2 Chronicles were written for the Jews returning from exile, many centuries after David, to encourage them by connecting them to their past. Their promise and hope for a restored Israel could be found in remembering what God did in their history—a history the people must remember and make their own.

Outline:

- Genealogies (1–9)
- David's victories (10–20)
- David's census (21–27)
- David's final days (28–29)

Key Verse: *God's promise to David: "I will set [your son] over my house and my kingdom forever."*
—1 Chronicles 17:14

2 CHRONICLES

The reigns of King Solomon and the kings of Judah

Written: c. 450–400 BC by an unknown author (possibly Ezra)

Purpose: To encourage the exiles who returned to Judah.

Summary: This book covers history from King Solomon all the way through the fall of Judah and the decree allowing the exiles to return home. This history is meant to inspire the people to remain faithful to God as he has been to them, and also to warn them about the consequences of complacency, rebellion, and idolatry.

Outline:

- King Solomon (1–9)
- Kings of Judah (10–35)
- Fall of Judah, exile, and the decree to return to Judah (36)

Key Verse: *"As for us, the LORD is our God, and we have not forsaken him."*
—2 Chronicles 13:10

KINGS OF ISRAEL AND JUDAH

The Kings of Israel (Northern Kingdom)

- ✘ Jeroboam I 931-910 [*1 Kings 11:26–14:20; 2 Chron. 9:29–13:20*]
- ✘ Nadab 910-909 [*1 Kings 15:25–31*]
- ✘ Baasha 909-886 [*1 Kings 15:27–16:7; 2 Chron. 16:1–6*]
- ✘ Elah 886-885 [*1 Kings 16:6–14*]
- ✘ Zimri 885 [*1 Kings 16:9–20*]
- ? Tibni 885-880 [*1 Kings 16:21–22*]
- ✘ Omri 885-874 [*1 Kings 16:15–28*]
- ✘ Ahab 874-853 [*1 Kings 16:28–22:40; 2 Chron. 18:1–34*]
- *1 Kings 22:40—2 Kings 1:18; 2 Chron. 20:35–37* ✘ Ahaziah 853-852
- *2 Kings 3:1–9:25; 2 Chron. 22:5–7* ✘ Joram (Jehoram) 852-841
- ✘ Jehu 841-814 [*2 Kings 9:1–10:36; 2 Chron. 22:7–9*]
- ✘ Jehoahaz 814-798 [*2 Kings 13:1–9*]
- ✘ Jehoash 798-792 [*2 Kings 13:9–14:16; 2 Chron. 25:17–25*]
- *2 Kings 14:23–29* ✘ Jeroboam II 793-753
- *2 Kings 14:29–15:12* ✘ Zechariah 753
- *2 Kings 15:10–15* ✘ Shallum 752
- *2 Kings 15:14–22* ✘ Menahem 752-742
- *2 Kings 15:25–31; 2 Chron. 28:5–8* ✘ Pekah 752-732
- *2 Kings 15:22–26* ✘ Pekahiah 742-740
- *2 Kings 15:30–17:6* ✘ Hoshea 732-722

Northern kingdom falls to the Assyrian Empire 722 •

900 BC | 800 BC

The Kings of Judah (Southern Kingdom)

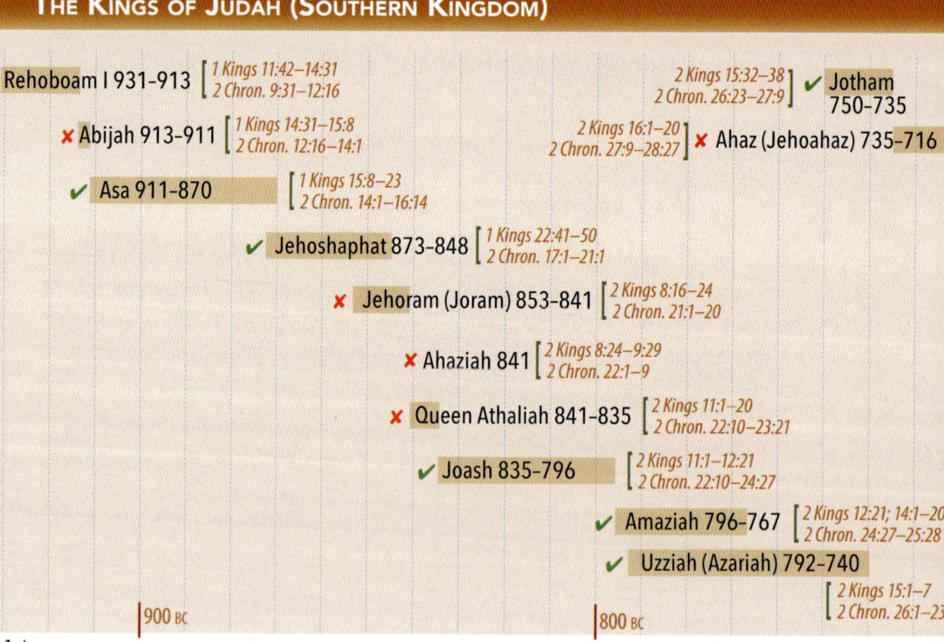

What made a king "good" or "bad"?

The biblical writers were not as interested in a king's abilities as an administrator as they were in the king's desire to follow God's commands. Kings that followed God's law and those who outlawed the altars to foreign gods, the high places, and idol worship were designated as good. Those who did not, were evil. The Bible uses the phrase "He did evil in the eyes (or sight) of the Lord," to evaluate the king's reign. In secular history, one of the important kings was Omri of Israel, who conquered the Moabites; but in the Bible this evil king's victories go unmentioned.

LEGEND

✔ = Good King

✘ = Bad King

? = No Record

700 BC | 600 BC | 500 BC

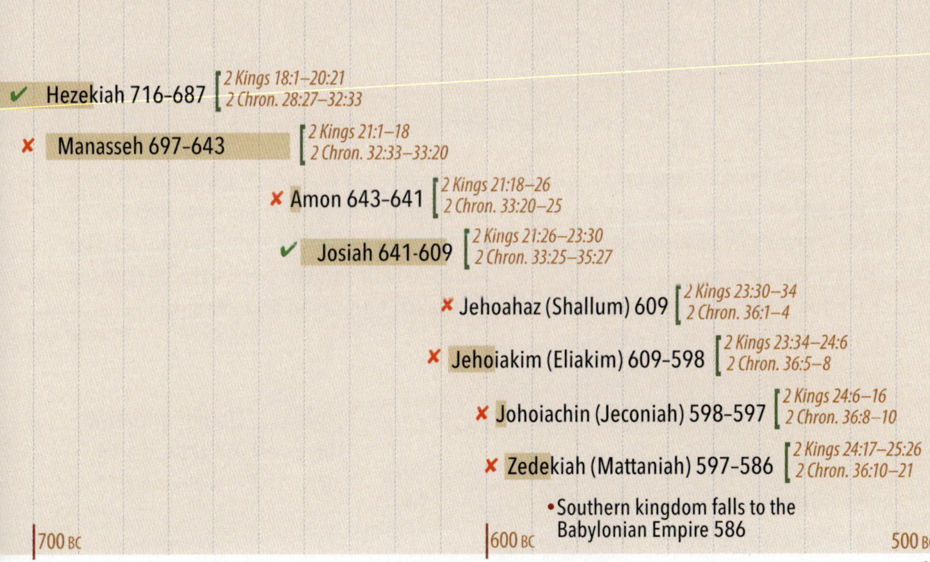

EZRA

History of the first and second waves of Jews who returned to Jerusalem

Written: c. 400s BC by Ezra

Purpose: To provide an account of the exiles' return and restoration.

Summary: The book of Ezra shows how God is faithful to his promise to restore his people. After they spend decades in exile in Babylon and Persia, King Cyrus of Persia allows the Jews to return to their homeland. The first wave of returning Jews is led by Zerubbabel who oversees the rebuilding of the temple in Jerusalem. The second wave is led by Ezra, a court scribe and priest, who guides the community in spiritual renewal.

Outline:

- First return led by Zerubbabel (1–2)
- The temple is rebuilt (3–6)
- Second return led by Ezra (7–8)
- Spiritual restoration (9–10)

Key Verse: *"[The LORD] is good; his love toward Israel endures forever."* —Ezra 3:11

NEHEMIAH

History of the third wave of Jews who returned to Jerusalem

Written: c. 400s BC by Ezra

Purpose: To provide an account of the exiles' return and restoration.

Summary: Originally one book with Ezra, the book of Nehemiah continues where Ezra left off. Nehemiah is a cupbearer to a Persian king who permits him to lead a group of Jews to Jerusalem to rebuild the crumbling walls of the city. This enormous task is completed in only 52 days despite much opposition. Whereas Ezra led a spiritual restoration, Nehemiah leads a political and physical restoration of Jerusalem and its inhabitants.

Outline:

- Third return led by Nehemiah (1–2)
- Rebuilding the walls (3)
- Threats and persecution (4–7)
- Renewal and dedication (8–13)

Key Verse: *"Do not grieve, for the joy of the LORD is your strength."* —Nehemiah 8:10

ESTHER

A story of courage in dangerous times

Written: c. 400s BC by an unknown author

Purpose: To demonstrate that in all circumstances God is in control.

Summary: The book of Esther is the story of a young Jewish woman thrown into a world of political intrigue and power plays in the Persian court in Susa. The story takes place while the Jews were in exile. Esther becomes queen to Persian King Xerxes I (Ahasuerus). She makes courageous choices to save her people from being slaughtered by their enemies.

Although the book does not mention God directly, his hand is seen throughout the story. The book of Esther offers reassurance that even when God seems to be absent from our world or suffering, he is ever present, interested, and ready to act.

Outline:

- Esther becomes queen (1–2)
- Haman's plot against the Jews (3)
- Esther's plan to protect her people (4–6)
- Haman's downfall (7)
- The Jews are saved and Purim is established (8–10)

Key Verse: *Mordecai said to Queen Esther: "And who knows but that you have come to your royal position for such a time as this?"* —Esther 4:14

Purim is an annual holiday commemorating God's deliverance of the Jewish people from Haman's evil plans (Esther 9:28). Today, Purim is celebrated with a reading of the book of Esther, noisemakers called groggers, hamantashen ("Haman's hat") cookies, and other festivities.

JOB

A story of suffering and trust

Written: Date and author are unknown.

Purpose: To show the sovereignty of God and to illustrate faithfulness in the midst of suffering.

Summary: Though the story of Job is set in an unknown place called Uz somewhere in Mesopotamia probably around the time of Abraham, its themes of human suffering and God's wisdom are timeless. While the beginning and end parts of Job are written in prose—the common way people speak and write—the bulk of the book is poetry.

In the story, Job is a "blameless and upright" (1:1) man who, unaware of the conversations happening in the celestial court between God and Satan, finds his life overturned. When Job loses everything, his friends try to make sense of his suffering by blaming him, and his wife tells him to curse God. Yet through all his intense pain, Job does "not sin by charging God with wrongdoing" (1:22).

In God's answer at the end of the book, Job is reminded that God is sovereign over all creation. Human wisdom can never fully fathom God's ways. Most often, we cannot see or understand his rule behind the scenes. But like Job, during times of suffering, we can still put our trust in a sovereign and compassionate God who loves and cares for us.

Outline:

Prose: Job tested by losing everything (1–2)

Poetry: Dialogues (3–41)

- Job and his friends: Eliphaz, Bildad, Zophar (3–27)
- A poem about wisdom (28)
- Job's final speech to his friends (29–31)
- Elihu's speech (32–37)
- God's answer to Job (38–41)

Prose: Job restored (42)

Key Verse: *"I know that my redeemer lives, and that in the end he will stand on the earth. And after my skin has been destroyed, yet in my flesh I will see God."*
—Job 19:25–26

PSALMS

A collection of poetic songs

Written: c. 1000–450 BC by David (73 psalms), Asaph (12 psalms), sons of Korah (11 psalms), and others

Purpose: To communicate with God and worship him.

Summary: The book of Psalms is a collection of songs (psalms) written and compiled over a long time span. It can be separated into five collections (books).

Because the psalms are poetry, they have a wonderful way of expressing our hearts. How do we approach a holy and awesome God? The psalms show us how to worship and pray to God. What words can we use to bring to God our most deeply felt emotions? The psalms provide us with the vocabulary.

Outline:

Book	Psalms	Themes
1	1–41	Prayers of lament and expressions of confidence in God's salvation.
2	42–72	Community laments. The book ends with a royal psalm.
3	73–89	Prayers of lament and distress more intense and bleak than in books 1 and 2.
4	90–106	The Lord reigns! Book 4 presents the answers to the bleakness of book 3.
5	107–150	God is in control, faithful, and good. He will redeem his people.

Key Verse: *"My mouth will speak in praise of the LORD. Let every creature praise his holy name for ever and ever."* —Psalms 145:21

Old Testament Hebrew poetry is written in short lines with lots of parallelism and metaphors. Poetry has a unique ability to voice deep feelings and thoughts beautifully, making it a perfect instrument to express the timeless wisdom found in the books of Job, Psalms (shown here), Proverbs, Ecclesiastes, and Song of Songs.

PROVERBS

Wisdom for godly living

Written: c. 900s–700s BC by King Solomon and others

Purpose: To gain wisdom and instruction for prudent behavior and doing what is right (1:1–3).

Summary: The book of Proverbs invites readers to make life-changing decisions between wisdom and foolishness. The readers "hear" from both Lady Wisdom and Lady Folly (Foolishness). Their invitations become alternatives between a path of wisdom that leads to life and a path of foolishness that leads to death. How do we start down the road of wisdom? Proverbs 9:10 answers: "The fear of the LORD is the beginning of wisdom."

When reading Proverbs, remember that biblical proverbs are not guarantees for a secure and successful life, nor are they universal or always applicable. Proverbs are not adequate for every occasion, but are limited by good timing for their use (26:9; 15:23).

Outline:

- Invitations to choose wisdom or foolishness (1–9)
- Proverbs of Solomon (10–21)
- Thirty sayings and other wise words (22–24)
- Solomon's sayings (25–29)
- Words of Agur and Lemuel (30:1–31:9)
- Poem of the wise woman (31:10–31)

Key Verse: *"Trust in the LORD with all your heart and lean not on your own understanding; in all your ways submit to him, and he will make your paths straight."—Proverbs 3:5–6*

"God gave Solomon wisdom and very great insight, and a breadth of understanding as measureless as the sand on the seashore" (1 Kings 4:29).

ECCLESIASTES

Searching for meaning and truth

Written: c. 971–931 BC by King Solomon or possibly by different authors later in the 500s BC

Purpose: To examine what a meaningful life is.

Summary: The author of Ecclesiastes (Greek for "one who speaks in an assembly") wants to make sense out of life, wisdom, and truth. At first, he proposes that everything is meaningless (vanity). After careful observation, the pursuit of all worldly pleasures, an assessment of wisdom, and an analysis of the purpose of life, he concludes that a meaningful life is not found in the frivolous pursuit of wealth, success, and pleasure. Instead, it is found in pursuing God as our number one priority, remembering and obeying our Creator.

Outline:

- Everything is meaningless (1–2)
- A time for everything (3–5)
- Life is not always fair (6–10)
- Remember and obey God (11–12)

Key Verse: *"Fear God and keep his commandments, for this is the duty of all mankind."*
—Ecclesiastes 12:13

SONG OF SONGS

A love song

Written: c. 971–931 BC by King Solomon and possibly others as late as the 500s BC

Purpose: To illustrate the joy of authentic love found in marriage.

Summary: Song of Songs (or Song of Solomon) is a collection of love poems declaring mutual love and affection between the lover and his beloved. Rather than writing from his own marital experience—Solomon had 700 wives and 300 concubines (1 Kings 11:3)!—the poems are written to present us with the way things should be within a loving, covenant relationship.

Outline:

- Courtship (1–2)
- Wedding (3–4)
- Loving relationship (5–8)

Key Verse: *"I am my beloved's and my beloved is mine."*
—Song of Songs 6:3

ISAIAH

Judgment and salvation

Written: c. 735–681 BC by the prophet Isaiah

Purpose: To convince the people that salvation is possible through repentance for sin and hope in the coming Messiah.

Summary: With powerful enemies on all sides and war looming, God's people formed political and military alliances with pagan nations in hopes of protecting themselves. Isaiah opposes these alliances because they show reliance on human power over God's power. In ancient times, nations that became subject to more powerful ones would adopt the gods and religious practices of their overlords. God commissions the prophet Isaiah to bring messages of impending judgment if God's people continue to look for their salvation in the strength and gods of other nations.

Outline:

Condemnation (1–39)

- Judgment for Judah (1–5)
- Isaiah's commission (6)
- Branch from Jesse (11–12)
- Prophecies against nations (13–35)
- Coming Babylonian exile (36–39)

Comfort in exile (40–55)

- Restoration of Israel (40–48)
- Suffering Servant (Messiah) (49–55)

Future hope (56–66)

- Salvation (56–57)
- Everlasting kingdom of God (58–66)

Key Verse: *"For to us a child is born, to us a son is given, and the government will be on his shoulders. And he will be called Wonderful Counselor, Mighty God, Everlasting Father, Prince of Peace."* —Isaiah 9:6

The Taylor Prism, made around 689 BC and discovered in Nineveh (in modern day Iraq), details the military campaign of King Sennacherib of Assyria against King Hezekiah of Judah boasting that he had Hezekiah "like a bird in a cage." This discovery shows the turmoil and danger God's people faced.

JEREMIAH

Judgment, wrath, and weeping

Written: c. 626–582 BC by the prophet Jeremiah

Purpose: To warn the people of destruction and to remind them of their sin in hopes of bringing them to repentance.

Summary: Jeremiah, who reluctantly obeys God's calling to be a prophet, brings a message of judgment against the people of Judah. He hopes that heartfelt repentance by God's people will deter God's wrath.

Outline:

- Jeremiah's call and message of judgment (1–10)
- Warnings of disaster and exile (11–28)
- New covenant and restoration (29–39)
- Fall of Jerusalem (40–52)

Key Verse: *"For I know the plans I have for you, . . . plans to prosper you and not to harm you, plans to give you hope and a future."* —Jeremiah 29:11

LAMENTATIONS

Dirge poem (lament)

Written: c. 586 BC by the prophet Jeremiah

Purpose: To express the despair of the people of Judah over the loss of their land, city, and temple.

Summary: Lamentations is an eyewitness account of the destruction of Jerusalem. The grief expressed in these poems reveals the deep regret and desire for the restoration of God's people.

Outline:

- Sorrow of captives (1)
- Anger with Jerusalem (2)
- Hope and mercy (3)
- Punishment (4)
- Restoration (5)

Key Verse: *"His compassions never fail. They are new every morning; great is your faithfulness."* —Lamentations 3:22–23

EZEKIEL

Prophecies and visions of God's presence

Written: c. 593–571 BC by the prophet Ezekiel

Purpose: To call God's people in exile to be faithful to God who is still among them.

Summary: The book of Ezekiel asks a crucial question: *Is God present with us or has he abandoned us?* Ezekiel, a temple priest in Jerusalem, was taken captive in 597 BC to Babylonia where he lived among other exiles. As captives in a foreign land, the people of God faced many daunting circumstances. Through prophecies and visions (some very unusual), Ezekiel communicates God's message that if the exiles were to walk humbly with God, then God's presence with them would be a source of peace, life, and future restoration.

Outline:

Call of Ezekiel (1–3)

Coming captivity of Judah (4–24)

- Judgment against Israel (4–7)
- Temple vision (8–11)
- God's judgment (12–24)

Judgment of other nations (25–32)

- Judah's neighbors (25)
- Tyre and Egypt (26–32)

Restoration of God's people (33–48)

- Fall of Jerusalem (33)
- Shepherds and sheep (34)
- Edom and Israel (35–37)
- Gog and Magog (38–39)
- Vision of restoration (40–48)

Similar imagery in the books of Ezekiel and Revelation

Image	Ezekiel	Revelation
Living creatures; God's throne	1:4–28	4:1–11
Eating a scroll	2:9–3:15	19:1–11
God's glory; temple	10:1–22	11:19
An adulterous woman	16:1–59; 23:1–49	17:1–18:24
Gog and Magog	38:1 – 39:29	20:7–10
New Jerusalem	40:1 – 48:35	21:1–22:6

Key Verse: *"I will give you a new heart and put a new spirit in you; I will remove from you your heart of stone and give you a heart of flesh."* —Ezekiel 36:26

DANIEL

Life in exile and visions of the future

Written: c. 605–535 BC by the prophet Daniel

Purpose: To convince the exiles that God is sovereign and to provide them with a vision of their future redemption.

Summary: The first part of the book tells about Daniel and his friends in the Babylonian court. This account shows God's people how to obey God while in the midst of a foreign, hostile land.

The second part of the book includes Daniel's visions that tell about future world events. The purpose of these visions is to reassure God's people facing persecution that God is in control. God will do wonders that will dwarf anything he had done before!

Outline:

Daniel and his friends (1–6)

- In the Babylonian court (1)
- Nebuchadnezzar's dream of the statue (2)
- Shadrach, Meshach, and Abednego (3)
- Nebuchadnezzar's dream of the tree (4)
- Belshazzar and the fall of Babylon (5)
- Daniel in the lion's den (6)

Daniel's visions (7–12)

- Four beasts and the Son of Man (7)
- Ram and he-goat (8)
- Seventy sevens (9)
- Future of Israel (10–12)

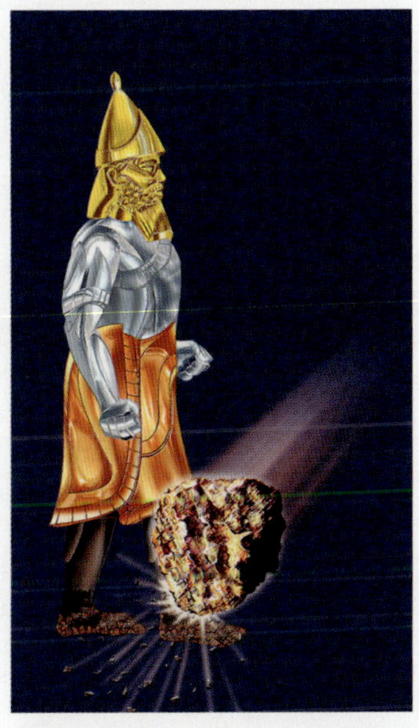

"There before you stood a large statue—an enormous, dazzling statue, awesome in appearance" (Daniel 2:31).

Key Verse: *"The God of heaven will set up a kingdom that will never be destroyed.... It will itself endure forever."* —Daniel 2:44

HOSEA

Warnings to a spiritually adulterous nation

Written: c. 752–722 BC by the prophet Hosea

Purpose: To illustrate Israel's spiritual adultery and warn of destruction.

Summary: Hosea is a prophet during the decline and fall of the Northern Kingdom of Israel. God commands him to marry an adulterous woman as a real-life illustration of God's never-failing love for the people of Israel who were being unfaithful to their covenant relationship with God.

Outline:

- Hosea and his unfaithful wife (1–3)
- Unfaithful Israel (4–10)
- God's love and anger (11–13)
- Israel's hope (14)

Key Verse: *"I desire mercy, not sacrifice, and acknowledgment of God rather than burnt offerings."*
—Hosea 6:6

JOEL

Prophecies about the great and dreadful day of the Lord

Written: possibly c. 500s–400s BC by the prophet Joel

Purpose: To call Judah to repentance in order to avoid judgment.

Summary: Joel warns God's people about the judgment they will face on the day of the Lord, but also of the amazing blessings God will pour out on those who heed the word of the Lord.

Outline:

- Locust plague (1:1–20)
- Army from the north (2:1–27)
- Day of the Lord (2:28–3:21)

Key Verse: *"I will pour out my Spirit on all people. Your sons and daughters will prophesy."*
—Joel 2:28 (See Acts 2:14–21)

AMOS

Warnings to a society gone awry

Written: c. 760–753 BC by the prophet Amos

Purpose: To accuse and judge Israel for injustice and lack of mercy.

Summary: Amos prophesies during a time of great material prosperity and peace. The people have become apathetic toward God, corrupting their worship and treating the poor unjustly. Amos, a shepherd from a small village, is sent by God to tell the people to change their ways or else face the judgment of God.

Outline:

- Israel and its neighbors (1–4)
- Call to repentance (5:1–17)
- False religion, injustice, pride (5:18–6:14)
- Judgment and restoration (7–9)

Key Verse: *"Seek good, not evil, that you may live. Then the LORD God Almighty will be with you."* —Amos 5:14

OBADIAH

A vision against Edom

Written: c. 586 BC by the prophet Obadiah

Purpose: To prophesy against Edom.

Summary: Obadiah, the shortest book in the Old Testament, judges the people of Edom for their disregard and mistreatment of the Israelites in Judah. Edom was a small kingdom southwest of the Dead Sea with a long history of hostility with Israel. In time, the Babylonian empire destroyed Edom.

Outline (verses):

- Judgment of Edom (1–9)
- Edom's violations (10–14)
- Israel's victory (15–21)

Key Verse: *"Because of the violence against your brother Jacob [the Israelites]...you will be destroyed forever."* —Obadiah 10

JONAH

A story of God's mercy

Written: c. 783–753 BC by the prophet Jonah

Purpose: To show that God loves all people.

Summary: It takes a storm, a great fish, and God's relentless pursuit of Jonah to get him to obey God's call for him to prophesy in the wicked and dangerous city of Nineveh. When Jonah does go to Nineveh, the Ninevites repent and God spares them from wrath. God's mercy extends to all people, even those who appear beyond redemption.

Outline:

- Jonah flees from God (1)
- Jonah prays inside the great fish (2)
- Jonah prophesies in Nineveh (3)
- Jonah resents God's mercy (4)

Key Verse: *"You are a gracious and compassionate God, slow to anger and abounding in love."*—Jonah 4:2

The Assyrians, whose capital was Nineveh, were known as ruthless military conquerors. Israel, like other small kingdoms, held no love for the Assyrians.

MICAH

A call to seek justice, love mercy, and walk humbly

Written: c. 738–698 BC by the prophet Micah

Purpose: To warn people of God's judgment and to offer hope.

Summary: Micah prophesies against the leaders of his people for their injustice, greed, and pride. Micah brings word of the destruction of Samaria and Jerusalem, but also proclaims a vision of future redemption and forgiveness.

Outline:

- Judgment and deliverance (1–5)
- Confession and restoration (6–7)

Key Verse: *"What does the LORD require of you? To act justly and to love mercy and to walk humbly with your God."* —Micah 6:8

NAHUM

Prophecy about the destruction of Nineveh

Written: c. 663–612 BC by the prophet Nahum

Purpose: To pronounce judgment on Nineveh.

Summary: God calls Nahum to warn about judgment against the Assyrian capital of Nineveh for their cruelty and idolatry. Though God is slow to anger, he will avenge his people for the atrocities Assyria committed against them. In 612 BC, Nahum's prophecy was fulfilled when Assyria fell to the Babylonian Empire.

Outline:

- Mercy and justice (1)
- Nineveh will fall (2)
- Woe to Nineveh (3)

Key Verse: *"The Lord is slow to anger but great in power; the Lord will not leave the guilty unpunished."* —Nahum 1:3

HABAKKUK

A prophet asks God about justice and mercy

Written: c. 609–598 BC by the prophet Habakkuk

Purpose: To affirm that the wicked will not prevail in the end.

Summary: Habakkuk asks the question: *Why does God let people get away with evil?* Habakkuk grapples with how God's anger and justice relate to his love and mercy. At the end of the book, Habakkuk recognizes that no matter what doubts he has, he knows that God will always render a righteous judgment in the end.

Outline:

- First complaint and answer (1:1–11)
- Second complaint and answer (1:12–2:20)
- Prayer of praise (3:1–19)

Key Verse: *"I will rejoice in the Lord, I will be joyful in God my Savior."* —Habakkuk 3:18

ZEPHANIAH

Warnings about judgment on the day of the Lord

Written: c. 641–628 BC by the prophet Zephaniah

Purpose: To motivate Judah to repentance.

Summary: Zephaniah prophesies during the reign of King Josiah, the last of Judah's good kings, who instituted spiritual reforms among the people. Zephaniah proclaims that the doom of the day of the Lord would be devastating to Judah and their neighbors unless they repent. He urges them to act quickly!

Outline:

- The day of the Lord (1)
- Judgment on Judah and other nations (2)
- A remnant restored (3)

Key Verse: *"The great day of the LORD is near—near and coming quickly."* —Zephaniah 1:14

HAGGAI

A message to rebuild the temple

Written: c. 520 BC by the prophet Haggai

Purpose: To urge the people to complete rebuilding the temple.

Summary: In Haggai's time, the Jews had returned to Jerusalem after 70 years of exile. At first they enthusiastically began rebuilding the temple, but soon fell into apathy. God's message through Haggai challenges the people to give careful thought to their ways and complete the task at hand because God is with them. The temple was completed four years later in 516 BC.

Outline:

- Rebuild the temple (1)
- Be strong, be holy, be blessed (2)

Key Verse: *"Is it a time for you yourselves to be living in your paneled houses, while [the Lord's] house remains a ruin? Give careful thought to your ways."* —Haggai 1:4–5

The Temple Mount in Jerusalem where the temple once stood

ZECHARIAH

Visions and messages about the Lord's reign over all

Written: c. 520–518 BC by the prophet Zechariah

Purpose: To give hope to the remnant in Israel.

Summary: Zechariah, a prophet of priestly lineage, travelled to Jerusalem from exile with the group who returned under governor Zerubbabel. Along with the prophet Haggai, Zechariah encourages the people to rebuild the temple. Zechariah's visions and messages of hope look forward to a time when God's reign will be recognized throughout the world.

Outline:

- Visions and messages (1–8)
- Oracles against the nations (9–14)

Key Verse: *"'Not by might nor by power, but by my Spirit,' says the LORD Almighty."* —Zechariah 4:6

MALACHI

The coming day of the Lord

Written: c. 400s BC by the prophet Malachi

Purpose: To examine Judah's actions and make sure God has priority.

Summary: Malachi calls for spiritual renewal among a people who had largely given up on God. The people had returned from exile and completed rebuilding the temple, but the blessings that Haggai and Zechariah prophesied about had yet to materialize. The people began to doubt God's blessings. With six prophetic speeches, Malachi urges the people to recognize their own unfaithfulness—shorting tithes, bringing unacceptable sacrifices, ignoring God's law— because the day of reckoning, the day of the Lord is coming.

Outline:

- Six prophetic speeches (1–3)
- The day of the Lord (4)

Key Verse: *"Bring the whole tithe into the storehouse . . . and see if I will not throw open the floodgates of heaven and pour out so much blessing."* —Malachi 3:10

TEMPLE TIME LINE

The temple (and earlier the tabernacle) was the place where God met with his people. It was a visible expression of God's desire to dwell among his people.

TABERNACLE

1446 BC
Exodus 25:8–9

Moses builds a portable tabernacle in the wilderness. The ark of the covenant is placed behind the veil, inside the Most Holy Place of the tabernacle.

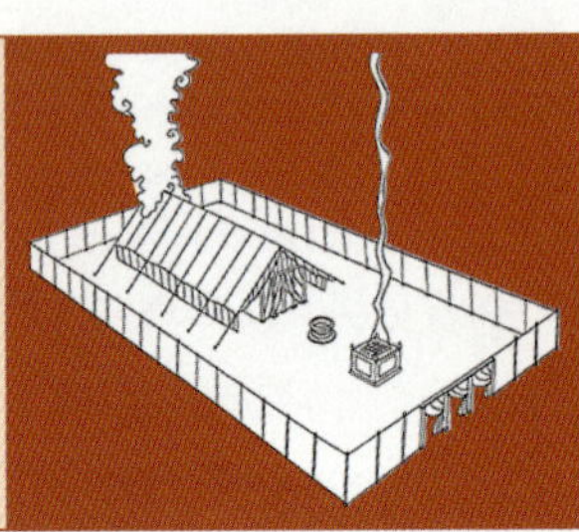

KING DAVID

1005 BC
2 Samuel 6:1–2; 24:21

King David brings the ark of the covenant into Jerusalem. David purchases a threshing floor on Mt. Moriah, the site where the temple would later be built.

SOLOMON'S TEMPLE

960 BC
1 Kings 6:1; 8:6

King Solomon builds the first temple in Jerusalem on Mt. Moriah and places the ark of the covenant in the Most Holy Place of the temple.

BABYLONIAN DESTRUCTION

586 BC
2 Kings 25:8–9

The Babylonians conquer Jerusalem and set fire to the temple. The whereabouts of the ark of the covenant from this point forward are unknown.

ZERUBBABEL'S TEMPLE

516 BC

Ezra 3:11–12

Under the leadership of Zerubbabel, the Jews return from exile and rebuild the temple in Jerusalem, but it is not as glorious as the previous temple.

HEROD'S TEMPLE

20 BC

King Herod begins a massive expansion of the Temple Mount.

JESUS

c. 4 BC–AD 29

Luke 2:25–38; Mark 11:15; 12:35; 15:38

- At the temple, Simeon and Anna recognize the infant Jesus as the Messiah.
- In the temple courtyards, Jesus teaches his followers, heals the sick, and confronts the money changers.
- When Jesus dies on the cross, the thick veil of the Most Holy Place in the temple is torn in half, signifying that Jesus' death opens a way for all people to commune with God.

ROMAN DESTRUCTION

AD 70

To quell an uprising, the Romans massacre thousands in Jerusalem and destroy the temple.

PRESENT DAY

Today, the Temple Mount is the site of the Islamic Dome of the Rock, the al-Aqsa Mosque, and the Western Wall.

NEW TESTAMENT

Gospels & Acts

Matthew through Acts – 5 books

The four Gospels record the good news (gospel) of God's plan for a Savior through the life, ministry, death, and resurrection of Jesus Christ. Each writer has a particular method or style to communicate the life and message of Jesus.

Acts is the record of the radically changed actions (or acts) of the followers of Jesus after his return to heaven. The book opens with the out-flowing of the Holy Spirit and describes the missionary efforts of the early followers of Jesus as they spread the gospel.

Paul's Epistles

Romans through Philemon – 13 books

These letters (called epistles) are written by the apostle Paul to young churches, pastors, and friends to guide, encourage, and correct them as they live as followers of Jesus.

General Epistles & Revelation

Hebrews through Revelation – 9 books

These letters are written by early church leaders—such as Peter John, and James—to provide encouragement to Christians facing persecution and to warn them about false teachings.

Revelation is addressed to seven churches in Asia Minor (Turkey today) and is written in an apocalyptic style, revealing God's plan for humanity through vivid signs, symbols, and visions.

MIRACLES OF JESUS

Miracle	Matthew	Mark	Luke	John
Healing				
Man with Leprosy	8:1-4	1:40-45	5:12-15	
Centurion's Servant	8:5-13		7:1-10	
Peter's Mother-in-law	8:14-15	1:29-31	4:38-9	
Cast out Demons	8:28-34	5:1-20	8:26-39	
Paralyzed Man	9:1-8	2:1-12	5:17-26	
Woman with Hemorrhage	9:20-22	5:25-34	8:43-48	
Two Blind Men	9:27-31			
Mute, Demon-Possessed Man	9:32-33		11:14	
Man with Shriveled Hand	12:9-13	3:1-5	6:6-10	
Blind, Mute, Possessed Man	12:22-23			
Canaanite Woman's Daughter	15:21-28	7:24-30		
Boy with a Demon	17:14-21	9:14-29	9:37-42	
Blind (Bartimaeus)	20:29-34	10:46-52	18:35-43	
Deaf Mute		7:31-37		
Possessed Man in Synagogue		1:21-28	4:31-37	
Blind Man at Bethsaida		8:22-26		
Crippled Woman			13:10-17	
Man with Dropsy			14:1-4	
Ten Lepers			17:11-19	
High Priest's Servant			22:49-51	
Official's Son				4:46-54
Sick Man at Pool of Bethesda				5:1-15
Man Born Blind				9:1-41
Power Over Nature				
Calming the Storm	8:23-27	4:35-41	8:22-25	
Feeding the 5,000	14:13-21	6:32-44	9:10-17	6:1-13
Walking on Water	14:22-33	6:45-51		6:16-21
Feeding the 4,000	15:29-38	8:1-9		
Coin in Fish	17:24-27			
Fig Tree Withered	21:18-22	11:12-14, 20-25		
Large Catch of Fish			5:4-11	
Water Turned to Wine				2:1-11
Another Large Catch of Fish				21:1-11
Raising the Dead				
Jairus's Daughter	9:18-19, 23-26	5:21-24, 35-43	8:40-42, 49-56	
Widow's Son			7:11-17	
Lazarus				11:1-44

PARABLES OF JESUS

Parable	Matthew	Mark	Luke
Lamp under a Bowl	5:14-16	4:21-22	8:16-17; 11:33-36
Wise and Foolish Builders	7:24-27		6:46-49
New Cloth on an Old Garment	9:16	2:21	5:36
New Wine in Old Wineskins	9:17	2:22	5:37-38
Sower and the Seeds	13:3-8, 18-23	4:3-8, 13-20	8:5-8, 11-15
Weeds in the Field	13:24-30, 36-43		
Mustard Seed	13:31-32	4:30-32	13:18-19
Yeast	13:33		13:20-21
Hidden Treasure	13:44		
Valuable Pearl	13:45-46		
Net of Good and Bad Fish	13:47-50		
Owner of a House	13:52		
Lost Sheep	18:12-14		15:4-7
Unmerciful Servant	18:23-35		
Workers in the Vineyard	20:1-16		
Two Sons	21:28-32		
Evil Tenants	21:33-44	12:1-11	20:9-18
Wedding Banquet	22:2-14		14:16-24
Fig Tree	24:32-35	13:28-31	21:29-33
Faithful vs. Wicked Servant	24:45-51		12:42-48
Ten Bridesmaids	25:1-13		
Talents	25:14-30		19:12-27
Sheep and Goats	25:31-46		
Growing Seed		4:26-29	
Watchful Servants		13:32-37	12:35-40
Money Lender			7:41-43
Good Samaritan			10:30-37
Friend in Need			11:5 8
Rich Fool			12:16-21
Unfruitful Fig Tree			13:6-9
Lowest Seat at the Feast			14:7-14
Cost of Discipleship			14:28-33
Lost Coin			15:8-10
Prodigal Son			15:11-32
Shrewd Manager			16:1-13
Rich Man and Lazarus			16:19-31
Master and His Servant			17:7-10
Persistent Widow			18:2-8
Pharisee and Tax Collector			18:9-14

PROPHECIES FULFILLED BY JESUS

Prophecy	Old Testament Reference	New Testament Fulfillment
Be born of a woman and crush the serpent's (Satan's) head	Genesis 3:14-15	Hebrews 2:14; 1 John 3:8
Be a descendant of Abraham and a blessing to all nations	Genesis 18:17-18	Acts 3:25-26
Be of the tribe of Judah	Genesis 49:8-10	Hebrews 7:14; Revelation 5:5
Be born in Bethlehem	Micah 5:2-5	Matthew 2:1-6
Be born a king in the line of King David	Isaiah 9:7; 2 Samuel 7:12-13	Matthew 1:1; Luke 1:32
Be born of a virgin	Isaiah 7:13-14	Luke 1:26, 35
Be called Immanuel ("God with us")	Isaiah 7:13-14	Matthew 1:22-23
Be called out of Egypt	Hosea 11:1	Matthew 2:13-15
Be rejected as a capstone	Psalm 118:22-23	Matthew 21:42
Cause the deaf to hear and the blind to see	Isaiah 29:18; 35:5	Matthew 11:5
Be a light to the Gentiles	Isaiah 42:6; 49:6	Luke 2:25-32; Acts 26:23
Institute a new everlasting covenant	Jeremiah 31:31-34	Luke 22:15-20
Be a prophet like Moses	Deuteronomy 18:15-19	Acts 3:18-22
Be anointed by God	Psalm 45:6-7	Hebrews 1:8-9
Minister in Galilee (Zebulun, Naphtali)	Isaiah 9:1-2	Matthew 4:12-16
Have the government on his shoulders	Isaiah 9:6-7	1 Corinthians 15:24-25
Bring freedom to the captives	Isaiah 61:1-2	Luke 4:16-21
Enter Jerusalem riding on a donkey	Zechariah 9:9	Matthew 21:4-11
Be despised and rejected by many	Isaiah 53:2-3	Luke 17:25; 23:18
Be hung upon a tree as a curse for us	Deuteronomy 21:23	Galatians 3:13
Be accused by false witnesses	Psalm 27:12; 35:11	Mark 14:55-59
Be lifted up as Moses lifted up a snake	Numbers 21:8-9	John 3:14-15
Be thirsty during his execution	Psalm 22:15	John 19:28
Be pierced for our sins	Zechariah 12:10; Isaiah 53:5	John 20:25-27
Soldiers will cast lots for his clothing	Psalm 22:18	John 19:23-24
Be the Passover Lamb with no broken bone	Exodus 12:46	John 19:31-36
Be buried with the rich	Isaiah 53:9	Matthew 27:57
Be raised from the dead	Psalm 16:8-11	Luke 24:6-8

✝ MATTHEW

Jesus, the promised Messiah

Written: c. AD 60 by Matthew (Levi), a tax collector and one of Jesus' twelve disciples, to a Jewish Christian audience.

Purpose: To show Jesus as the Son of David, the kingly Messiah who fulfills prophecy.

Summary: Matthew focuses on the many ways Jesus fulfilled Old Testament prophecies and God's grand plan of salvation for Israel and the world. The book shows how Jesus the Messiah (16:16) has preeminence over the law (5:21–28), temple (12:6), Sabbath (12:8), prophets (12:41), wisdom (12:42), and heaven and Earth (28:18). The word *Messiah* is derived from a Hebrew word meaning "anointed one;" in Greek, it's *Christ*. Most Jews at the time of Jesus expected the Messiah to be a military leader who would liberate them from the Romans. But Jesus was an unexpected Messiah. He did liberate people, but not from Rome; rather from sin and death.

Outline:

Preparing the way (1–4)

- Birth (1–2)
- Baptism and temptation (3–4)

Jesus in Galilee (5–18)

- Sermon on the Mount (5–7)
- Miracles and teachings (8–15)
- Peter's confession of Christ (16)
- Transfiguration and teachings (17–18)

Jesus' last days in Judea and Jerusalem (19–27)

- Triumphal entry and controversies (19–25)
- Last Supper, Gethsemane, crucifixion (26–27)

Resurrection and Great Commission (28)

Mount Tabor in Galilee, the traditional site of Jesus' Transfiguration in Matthew 17:1–2.

Key Verse: *"Go and make disciples of all nations, baptizing them in the name of the Father and of the Son and of the Holy Spirit."* —Matthew 28:19 (The Great Commission)

MARK

Jesus, the suffering Son of Man

Written: c. AD 50s by John Mark, a disciple of Peter and a friend of Paul, to a Gentile (possibly Roman) Christian audience.

Purpose: To show Jesus as the suffering Son of Man sent to serve and not be served.

Summary: Jesus' first words in this book introduce the good news: "The kingdom of God has come near. Repent and believe the good news!" (1:15). Mark shows that the good news of God's rule over all things is revealed by Jesus' teachings and miracles. Jesus, the Son of Man, is God's active agent, his power in the world, and his means of defeating sin, death, and the devil. The title *Son of Man* is from Daniel 7:13–14 which expresses the promise of a king who would defeat the forces of evil and establish God's eternal kingdom. Yet Jesus, our kingly champion, appears in humility. Jesus shares in the suffering that probably many of Mark's original audience experienced in persecution for their faith.

Outline:

Beginning of Jesus' ministry (1)

- Jesus' baptism and temptation (1:1–13)
- Calling disciples (1:14–45)

Jesus' public ministry (2–10)

- Controversies with Jewish authorities (2–3)
- Teachings, miracles, and the kingdom of God (4–5)
- Jesus' ministry beyond Galilee (6–8)
- Teachings, miracles, and Jesus predicts his death (9–10)

In Jerusalem (11–16)

- Final teachings (11–13)
- Arrest, crucifixion, and resurrection (14–16)

Key Verse: *"For even the Son of Man did not come to be served, but to serve, and to give his life as a ransom for many."* —Mark 10:45

Zev Radovan

In 1968, the bones of young man who had been crucified during New Testament times were found in Jerusalem. A seven-inch nail was still embedded in the bone, showing the gruesome and painful way the Romans crucified people.

LUKE

Jesus, the Savior of the world

Written: c. AD 60–62 by Luke (also the author of Acts), likely a doctor and Gentile fellow traveller with Paul, to a Gentile audience.

Purpose: To show Jesus as the Savior of the world who has compassion for all people.

Summary: Luke emphasizes how the good news of Jesus is for everyone. Themes in Luke's Gospel include the presences and power of the Holy Spirit (who will take center stage in Luke's second book, Acts) (4:14); God's kingdom is here and belongs to his children (12:32); Jesus' care and help for the poor and disadvantaged (6:17–19); and the importance of praying (18:1), as Luke records more instances of prayer than the other three Gospels.

Outline:

Jesus' birth and childhood (1–2)

John the Baptist prepares the way (3–4)

Jesus in Galilee (5–9)
- Clashes with religious leaders (5)
- Teaches his disciples (6)
- Identity of Jesus, his miracles, and teachings (7–9)

Jesus on the way to Jerusalem (10–18)
- Miracles and teachings in Judea (10–13)
- Miracles and teachings in Perea (14–18)

Garden of Gethsemane where Jesus prayed to the Father, "Yet not my will, but yours be done" (Luke 22:42).

Jesus in Jerusalem (19–24)
- Triumphal entry, Olivet Discourse, Last Supper, Gethsemane (19–22)
- Crucifixion, resurrection, ascension (23–24)

Key Verse: *"I bring you good news that will cause great joy for all the people. Today in the town of David a Savior has been born to you; he is the Messiah, the Lord."*
—Luke 2:10–11

JOHN

Jesus, the Son of God

Written: c. AD 85–95 by John, one of Jesus' twelve disciples and the author of 1, 2, and 3 John and Revelation, to both a Jewish and Gentile audience of believers and non-believers alike.

Purpose: To show Jesus as the Son of God, the Word made flesh, who provides eternal life for all who believe in him.

Summary: Near the end of his Gospel, John tells us why he wrote about Jesus: "These are written that you may believe that Jesus is the Messiah, the Son of God, and that by believing you may have life in his name" (20:31). John's Gospel teaches us who Jesus is, and that by putting our faith in him we have eternal life. John includes many stories about Jesus that are not found in the other three Gospels. Central themes in John are love (3:35; 13:34), eternal life (3:16; 10:28), light and darkness (1:5; 8:12), and the world versus Jesus' kingdom (18:36).

Outline:

The Word of God (the Son) becomes flesh (1)

First year of Jesus' ministry (first Passover) (2–4)

- First miracle, cleansing the temple (2)
- Nicodemus, Samaritan woman (3–4)

Second year of Jesus' ministry (second Passover) (5)

- Healing at the pool (5:1–15)
- Opposition and more miracles (5:16–47)

Third year of Jesus' ministry (third Passover) (6–11)

- Bread, water, light, "I am" statements (6–8)
- Healings, Good Shepherd, eternal life (9–11)

Last Passover (12–19)

- Triumphal entry (12)
- Prayer for his disciples, promises the Holy Spirit (13–17)
- Arrest, trial, crucifixion (18–19)

Resurrection and appearances of Jesus (20–21)

Recently discovered steps of the Pool of Siloam where Jesus sent a blind man to be healed in John 9. The pool dates back to the 1st century BC and was used during Jesus' time.

Key Verse: *"For God so loved the world that he gave his one and only Son, that whoever believes in him shall not perish but have eternal life."* —John 3:16

ACTS

The story of the early church

Written: c. AD 60–62 by Luke (also the author of the Gospel of Luke), likely a doctor and Gentile fellow traveller with Paul, to a Gentile audience.

Purpose: To record how the Holy Spirit acted through believers to spread the Word of God.

Summary: The book of Acts picks up where the Gospel of Luke left off, with Jesus' resurrection and then ascension into heaven. Acts tells the story of what the disciples did as a response to Jesus' commissioning them to be his witnesses (Acts 1:4–5, 8). The events in Acts show how the work of the Holy Spirit in the lives of believers (the church) spreads the good news of salvation in Jesus. The book of Acts begins in Jerusalem and ends in Rome.

Outline:

Mission in Jerusalem (1–7)
- Ascension of Jesus and the coming of the Holy Spirit (1–2)
- Ministry of Peter (3–5)
- Ministry of Stephen (6–7)

Mission in Judea and Samaria (8–12)
- Ministry of Philip (8)
- Saul's conversion (9)
- Peter and Cornelius (10–12)

Mission beyond Israel (13–28)
- Paul's first missionary journey (13–14)
- Paul's second missionary journey (15–18)
- Paul's third missionary journey (19–26)
- Paul's journey to Rome (27–28)

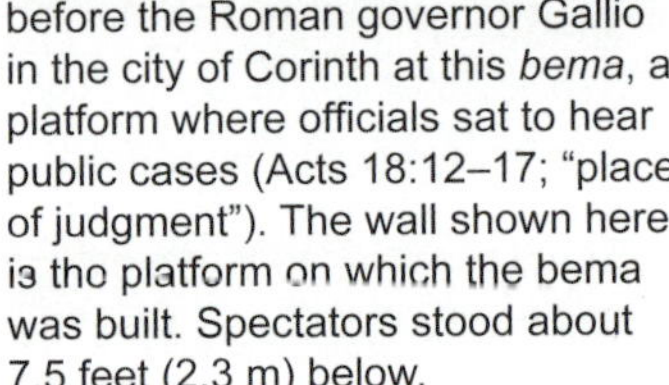

The apostle Paul was brought before the Roman governor Gallio in the city of Corinth at this *bema*, a platform where officials sat to hear public cases (Acts 18:12–17; "place of judgment"). The wall shown here is the platform on which the bema was built. Spectators stood about 7.5 feet (2.3 m) below.

Key Verse: *"But you will receive power when the Holy Spirit comes on you; and you will be my witnesses in Jerusalem, and in all Judea and Samaria, and to the ends of the earth."* —Acts 1:8

ROMANS

A letter about the power of the gospel

Written: c. AD 57 by the apostle Paul to Christians in Rome

Purpose: To teach about law, faith, salvation, and righteous living.

Summary: The epistle to the Romans is Paul's most theologically complex letter. It details crucial topics of the Christian faith. But it is also a personal letter. Paul sends greetings and encourages believers in Rome to be unified and live wisely. Though Paul had not yet visited the church in Rome, he hoped to make Rome his base for launching a missionary effort that would reach all the way to Spain.

Outline:

The power of the gospel (1–8)

- Condemnation (1–3)
- Sanctification (4–5)
- Glorification (6–8)

Israel and the gospel (9–11)

The gospel in believers' lives (12–16)

- Living sacrifices (12–13)
- The weak and strong (14–16)

Key Verse: *"Do not conform to the pattern of this world, but be transformed by the renewing of your mind."* —Romans 12:2

Paul eventually made it to Rome—but in chains! He travelled to Rome along part of the Appian Way (shown here). See Acts 28.

Paul's encounter with the risen Christ in Acts 9 put him on a radically new path. He went from fiercely persecuting Christians to becoming the greatest Christian missionary of all time. He authored more books of the Bible than anyone else. Paul's faith eventually cost him his life. According to tradition, Paul (along with the apostle Peter) was martyred in Rome under Emperor Nero's persecution of Christians in AD 64–68.

1 CORINTHIANS

A letter to clear up misunderstandings

Written: c. AD 55–56 by the apostle Paul to Christians in Corinth

Purpose: To address divisions and immorality in the church, and to encourage believers to love one another.

Summary: There was a lot of misunderstandings and confusion in the church at Corinth (5:9–10). Paul wrote this letter to answer questions about the many issues they faced, including Christian conscience, sexual conduct, spiritual gifts, love, and the resurrection.

Outline:

- Divisions (1–4)
- Morality (5–11)
- Doctrine (12–15)
- Final greetings (16)

Key Verse: *"Love is patient, love is kind. It does not envy, it does not boast, it is not proud."* —1 Corinthians 13:4

2 CORINTHIANS

Paul's most personal letter

Written: c. AD 56 by the apostle Paul to Christians in Corinth

Purpose: To defend Paul's call as an apostle and to address deceivers.

Summary: Second Corinthians is Paul's most personal epistle. In this letter, Paul reinforces what he wrote in 1 Corinthians and then offers a passionate defense of his ministry in the face of many attacks.

Outline:

- Apostleship (1–7)
- Sacrificial giving (8–9)
- False apostles (10–12)
- Final greetings (13)

Key Verse: *"My grace is sufficient for you, for my power is made perfect in weakness."* —2 Corinthians 12:9

Temple of Apollo in ancient Corinth, Greece

GALATIANS

A letter about justification by faith

Written: c. AD 48–49 by the apostle Paul to Christians in Galatia

Purpose: To warn against legalism and defend justification by faith.

Summary: Paul defends his authority as an apostle and argues that the true gospel teaches that justification is by faith alone, contrary to what some false preachers in the church were saying. He urges believers to use their freedom in Christ to walk in the Spirit and not in the sinful desires of the flesh.

Outline:

- Paul's defense (1–2)
- Justification by faith (3–4)
- Living by the Spirit (5–6)

Key Verse: *"The fruit of the Spirit is love, joy, peace, forbearance, kindness, goodness, faithfulness, gentleness and self-control."* —Galatians 5:22–23

EPHESIANS

A letter about living in God-honoring ways

Written: c. AD 60–62 by the apostle Paul to Christians in Ephesus

Purpose: To show believers what it means to be a follower of Christ and encourage them in their spiritual walk.

Summary: Writing from a prison in Rome, Paul encourages believers in Ephesus as they face tremendous pressure to participate in the sinfulness of their surroundings. Ephesus—a cosmopolitan city with Jews, Greeks, and Romans—was known for its many pagan cults, particularly the worship of the goddess Diana.

Outline:

- Grace (1)
- Reconciliation (2–3)
- Christian living (4–6)

Key Verse: *"For it is by grace you have been saved, through faith—and this is not from yourselves, it is the gift of God."* —Ephesians 2:8

PHILIPPIANS

A letter about living like Christ

Written: c. AD 60–62 by the apostle Paul to Christians in Philippi

Purpose: To express Paul's love and affection for believers.

Summary: Written while under house arrest in Rome, Paul urges believers to "have the same mind-set as Christ Jesus" (2:5) and learn to live humbly toward one another, so that there is unity in the church.

Outline:

- Paul's imprisonment (1)
- Living humbly like Christ (2)
- Encouragement to press on (3)
- Plea for unity (4)

Key Verse: *". . . being confident of this, that he who began a good work in you will carry it on to completion until the day of Christ Jesus."* —Philippians 1:6

COLOSSIANS

A letter about the supremacy of Christ

Written: c. AD 60–62 by the apostle Paul to Christians in Colossae

Purpose: To counteract false teachings about Christ and to encourage believers.

Summary: The church in Colossae was dealing with false teachings, including the legalism of requiring Gentile Christians to follow Jewish religious laws. Paul dispels the false teachings by emphasizing the supremacy of Christ over all human actions and philosophies.

Outline:

- Supremacy of Christ (1)
- Freedom in Christ (2)
- Christian living (3–4)

Key Verse: *"For in Christ all the fullness of the Deity lives in bodily form. . . . He is the head over every power and authority."* —Colossians 2:9–10

1 THESSALONIANS

A letter about hope in the face of persecution

Written: c. AD 50–52 by the apostle Paul to Christians in Thessalonica

Purpose: To express Paul's care for believers and to encourage them.

Summary: Paul and Silas, facing violent persecution in Thessalonica, were forced to flee the city (Acts 17:1–10). It is no wonder then, that Paul spends the first three chapters of this letter discussing his actions and absence. Paul then encourages believers to live holy lives, despite enduring persecution, because Christ is coming again.

Outline:

- Paul's actions and absence (1–3)
- Believers who have died (4)
- The day of the Lord (5)

Key Verse: *"For the Lord himself will come down from heaven . . . with the trumpet call of God, and the dead in Christ will rise first."* —1 Thessalonians 4:16

2 THESSALONIANS

A letter about being ready

Written: c. AD 50–52 by the apostle Paul to Christians in Thessalonica

Purpose: To stress the importance of being ready for Christ's return.

Summary: Written about six months after Paul's first letter to the Thessalonians, this second letter echoes many themes in the first. Paul also warns believers not to be idle because everyone must be prepared for Christ's return.

Outline:

- Thanksgiving and prayer (1)
- Standing firm (2)
- Warnings against laziness (3)

Key Verse: *"Stand firm and hold fast to the teachings we passed on to you."* —2 Thessalonians 2:15

1 TIMOTHY

Instructions for leading a church

Written: c. AD 62–66 by the apostle Paul to Timothy, a young pastor in Ephesus

Purpose: To remove false doctrine and suggest proper church leadership.

Summary: In this letter, Paul gives instructions to Timothy, a young pastor dealing with false teachings within the church in Ephesus.

Outline:

- Proper worship (1–3)
- Correct doctrine (4)
- Dealing with church members (5)
- Final instructions (6)

Key Verse: *"Don't let anyone look down on you because you are young, but set an example for the believers in speech, in conduct, in love, in faith and in purity."* —1 Timothy 4:12

2 TIMOTHY

A letter about persevering

Written: c. AD 66–67 by the apostle Paul to Timothy, a young pastor in Ephesus

Purpose: To encourage Timothy to remain faithful in ministry even in the midst of suffering.

Summary: Written from prison in Rome, this second letter to Timothy is perhaps Paul's last letter. Paul encourages the young pastor to persevere in preaching the gospel through hardships, and to hold fast to Scripture and guard the gospel against false teachings.

Outline:

- The gospel (1)
- False teachers (2)
- Preaching the word of God (3)
- Final instructions (4)

Key Verse: *"All Scripture is God-breathed and is useful for teaching, rebuking, correcting and training in righteousness."* —2 Timothy 3:16

Timothy, whose father was a Greek and mother a Jewish Christian, traveled with Paul on his second missionary journey (Acts 16:1–5). Paul spoke very highly of Timothy, saying, "I have no one else like him, who will show genuine concern for your welfare" (Philippians 2:20).

TITUS

Instructions for church leadership and upright living

Written: c. AD 64–66 by the apostle Paul to Titus, a pastor in Crete

Purpose: To encourage Christians to do good works.

Summary: Titus was a Gentile convert who travelled with Paul to Jerusalem (Galatians 2:1–5). Paul left Titus in charge of the churches on the island of Crete. This letter provides instructions about responsible church leadership, correct doctrine, and godly living.

Outline:

- Appointing elders (1)
- Doing good works (2–3)

Key Verse: *"God our Savior . . . saved us, not because of righteous things we had done, but because of his mercy."* —Titus 3:4–5

PHILEMON

An appeal for reconciliation

Written: c. AD 60–62 by the apostle Paul to Philemon in Colossae

Purpose: To ask Philemon to forgive and accept Onesimus.

Summary: Philemon, a leader in the church in Colossae, was the owner of a runaway slave named Onesimus. Later, after meeting Paul and becoming a Christian, Onesimus wanted reconciliation with his old master. This letter is a direct appeal from Paul to Philemon to accept Onesimus back "no longer as a slave, but . . . as a dear brother" (verses 15–16).

Outline (verses):

- Paul commends Philemon (1–7)
- Paul's appeal to Philemon (8–22)
- Final greetings (23–25)

Key Verse: *"Perhaps the reason he was separated from you for a little while was that you might have him back forever—no longer as a slave, but better than a slave, as a dear brother."* —Philemon 15–16

HEBREWS

A letter about the superiority of Christ

Written: c. AD 60–69 by an unknown author to a Jewish Christian audience

Purpose: To emphasize the superiority of Christ over the old covenant.

Summary: Jesus Christ is superior to the angels, the Old Testament prophets, Moses, the priesthood, and the sacrificial system. This is the message of Hebrews. Jesus' death on the cross fulfilled the Old Testament. Jesus leads his followers into God's rest, and this is a journey of faith (see chapter 11).

Outline:

- Supremacy of Christ (1–4)
- New covenant (5–10)
- The life of faith (11–13)

Key Verse: *"Let us run with perseverance the race marked out for us, fixing our eyes on Jesus, the pioneer and perfecter of faith."*
—Hebrews 12:1–2

JAMES

A letter about having a living faith

Written: c. AD 49 by James to a Jewish Christian audience

Purpose: To encourage believers to have faith that is active.

Summary: James addresses Christians who had become arrogant: showing favoritism to the wealthy, using their words to harm others, and failing to serve people in need. While salvation is by faith in Jesus, James reminds readers that having faith doesn't excuse anyone from living out that faith by doing the good things God has called them to do.

Outline:

- Perseverance (1)
- Favoritism (2:1–13)
- Faith and deeds (2:14–26)
- Words and wisdom (3)
- Humility (4)
- Patience and prayer (5)

James was the half-brother of Jesus (mentioned in Galatians 1:19) who was martyred in Jerusalem for his faith in AD 62.

Key Verse: *"As the body without the spirit is dead, so faith without deeds is dead."*
—James 2:26

1 PETER

A letter about suffering

Written: c. AD 64–65 by the apostle Peter to Christians in Asia Minor (modern-day Turkey)

Purpose: To call Christians to holy living even in the face of suffering.

Summary: As persecution of Christians increased in the time of the apostles, this letter encourages faithfulness and Christ-like behavior through very difficult circumstances.

Outline:

- Blessings (1)
- Relationships (2)
- Suffering (3)
- Holiness (4)
- Standing firm (5)

Key Verse: *"But just as he who called you is holy, so be holy in all you do."* —1 Peter 1:15

2 PETER

A letter about trusting the prophecies and promises of God

Written: c. AD 64–65 by the apostle Peter to Christians (possibly in Asia Minor)

Purpose: To urge believers not to waver in their faith.

Summary: This second letter warns believers against false teachers, encourages them to grow strong in their faith, and instructs them regarding the promised return of Jesus. Peter emphasizes that the prophetic word and apostolic testimony are not human creations, but are reliable testimonies.

Outline:

- Our calling (1)
- False teachers (2)
- Day of the Lord (3)

Key Verse: *"For prophecy never had its origin in the human will, but prophets, though human, spoke from God as they were carried along by the Holy Spirit."* —2 Peter 1:21

Peter, one of Jesus' twelve disciples, was a fisherman who became a top leader in the early church. It is believed that he was crucified for his faith during Emperor Nero's persecution of Christians in Rome around AD 64–68.

1 JOHN

A letter about love

Written: c. AD 85–95 by the apostle John to Christians in Asia Minor

Purpose: To emphasize Jesus' humanity and love.

Summary: The longest of John's three epistles, this letter focuses on love: God's love through Jesus and our love for one another. It also refutes false teachers who were claiming Jesus only *appeared* to be human. Jesus was in fact fully human—and fully God.

Outline:

- Light, love, and truth (1–3)
- Christ in the flesh (4)
- Keeping God's commands (5)

Key Verse: *"This is how we know what love is: Jesus Christ laid down his life for us. And we ought to lay down our lives for our brothers and sisters."* —1 John 3:16

2 JOHN

A letter about discernment

Written: c. AD 85–95 by the apostle John to "the lady chosen by God" (1:1), possibly an expression meaning "the church."

Purpose: To warn believers against falling into deception.

Summary: False teachers were corrupting the gospel by denying that Jesus came in the flesh. This short letter reminds believers that love, which means walking in God's commands, also includes being discerning so Christians will not deceived by false teachings.

Outline (verses):

- Love (1–6)
- False teachings (7–11)
- Final greetings (12–13)

Key Verse: *"And this is love: that we walk in obedience to his commands."* —2 John 6

John, the younger brother of the apostle James, was called the "disciple whom Jesus loved" (John 13:23). He wrote three epistles, the Gospel of John, and Revelation. Stories suggest that he died of natural causes in Ephesus around AD 100.

3 JOHN

A letter about loving others vs. loving to be first

Written: c. AD 85–95 by the apostle John to Gaius, a Christian in Asia Minor

Purpose: To praise Gaius for his loyalty and criticize Diotrephes for his pride.

Summary: This third letter—the shortest book in the New Testament—was written to commend Gaius for his love, faithfulness, and hospitality, but also to denounce Diotrephes for acting arrogantly, gossiping, and refusing to welcome other believers.

Outline (verses):

- John commends Gaius (1–8)
- John rebukes Diotrephes (9–10)
- Final greetings (11–14)

Key Verse: *"I have no greater joy than to hear that my children are walking in the truth."* —3 John 4

JUDE

A letter about contending for the faith

Written: AD 60s–80s (date unknown) by Jude to Christians everywhere

Purpose: To warn against false teachers.

Summary: Jude—Jesus' half-brother mentioned in Matthew 13:55 (aka "Judas")—penned this short letter to encourage believers to "contend for the faith" (verse 3). False teachers had come into the church seeking to "pervert the grace of our God into a license for immorality" (verse 4).

Outline (verses):

- Greetings (1–4)
- False teachers (5–19)
- Final greetings (20–25)

Key Verse: *"To him who is able to keep you from stumbling and to present you before his glorious presence without fault and with great joy."* —Jude 24

REVELATION

Visions that reveal God's glory and triumph

Written: c. AD 85–95 by the apostle John on the Island of Patmos to seven churches in Asia Minor (modern-day Turkey)

Purpose: To give hope to persecuted Christians and to provide a vision of Christ's return.

Summary: The book of Revelation describes the amazing visions the apostle John received while living in exile on the Island of Patmos. Christians in John's day faced severe persecution. The messages in Revelation remind believers that even when evil seems so strong, God is in control of history. God will ultimately defeat Satan and his forces. The Lord will renew his creation and live among his people. "He will wipe every tear from their eyes. There will be no more death or mourning or crying or pain, for the old order of things has passed away" (21:4).

Outline:

- Vision of Christ (1)
- Seven churches (2–3)
- Seven seals (4–7)
- Seven trumpets (8–11)
- Seven histories (12–14)
- Seven bowls (15–16)
- Fall of Babylon (17–18)
- Visions of the end (19–21)
- Invitation to come (22)

Revelation is almost exclusively *apocalyptic*, a word meaning "reveal, uncover." Apocalyptic literature reveals God's hidden plans through symbols and visions. The books of Daniel and Ezekiel also contain apocalyptic writings.

Key Verse: *"He who testifies to these things says, 'Yes, I am coming soon.' Amen. Come, Lord Jesus."* —Revelation 22:20

Island of Patmos